D0596411

Agent Angus

K.L. Denman

Orca currents

ORCA BOOK PUBLISHERS

Library and Archives Canada Cataloguing in Publication

Denman, K.L., 1975-
Agent Angus / K.L. Denman.
(Orca currents)

Issued also in electronic format.
ISBN 978-1-4598-0104-2 (bound).--ISBN 978-1-4598-0103-5 (pbk.)

I. Title. II. Series: Orca currents
PS8607.E64A64 2012   JC813'.6   C2011-907790-6

First published in the United States, 2012
Library of Congress Control Number: 2011943731

Summary: Angus and his best friend, Shahid, two smart misfits,
embark on a criminal investigation with comedic results.

*Orca Book Publishers is dedicated to preserving the environment and has
printed this book on paper certified by the Forest Stewardship Council®.*

Orca Book Publishers gratefully acknowledges the support for its
publishing programs provided by the following agencies: the Government
of Canada through the Canada Book Fund and the Canada Council for the Arts,
and the Province of British Columbia through the BC Arts Council
and the Book Publishing Tax Credit.

Cover photography by dreamstime.com

ORCA BOOK PUBLISHERS
PO Box 5626, Stn. B
Victoria, BC Canada
V8R 6S4

ORCA BOOK PUBLISHERS
PO Box 468
Custer, WA USA
98240-0468

www.orcabook.com
Printed and bound in Canada.

15 14 13 12 • 4 3 2 1

For Edie and Denny,
who always enjoy a chuckle.

Chapter One

I'm not a lucky guy. But today luck has chosen to place me next to the one and only Ella Eckles. It's like a miracle. We're standing on the school's front lawn, at the edge of a crowd of students. The school has been evacuated. A massive stink bomb in the main hall is still smoking.

I risk a furtive glance at Ella and see that her nose is wrinkled. It's a strong nose with a shapely profile. It always keeps her black-framed eyeglasses neatly in place. And clearly, it's a sensitive nose. True, my nose is wrinkling from the stench wafting from the school too. But my belief that Ella's nose is sensitive isn't based only on this moment. I know that she's artistic, and artists are sensitive in many ways.

Ella is carrying her sketchbook. She draws all the time. Maybe I could ask her what she's working on. Would that be cool? I think it would. I take a deep breath to prepare myself and almost gag.

Note to self: Avoid inhaling rude aromas.

I hear Ella ask, "Are you okay?"

I look to see who she's talking to and make direct eye contact with her. She's asking *me* if I'm okay.

I rally my voice and croak, "Yeah. It's just the…you know…"

"I know. The smell. So disgusting." Her eyes are warm brown. She's taller than me but not by much. Our glasses are almost dead level. "You're Angus, right?"

"You know my name?" Like an idiot, I say that out loud. Ella's lips curve into a small smile, and she nods.

"Oh. Wow. I know yours too. Ella Eckles. Ha ha."

Her smile fades. "You think my name is funny?"

"What? No. It's a beautiful name. Beautiful, like…" Do *not* say like a fulcrum point. Nor like Topio 3.0, the Ping-Pong-playing robot. I can't compare her name to things I usually call beautiful. I give up and say, "So. You're into drawing, huh?"

"Yeah." She hugs her sketchbook to her chest. She sure loves that thing.

"Sweet. So what do you draw?"

She looks down at her foot, prodding the grass. "You'll think it's dumb."

"No, I won't," I say. "Anything you—
I mean, I think creating art is, whoa.
Incredible."

She looks at me again. "Really?
You won't laugh?"

I shake my head.

She bites her lip for a second before
saying, "I want to be an animator.
For film or video games. So I draw
everything I see or imagine."

"Wow! An animator. That is *so* cool."
It really is. I want to say more, but I'm
experiencing a brain fart. Nothing
comes to me. Think, Angus, think.

"Would you like to see what I'm
working on?" she asks.

I respond with a huge nod.

She gives me that little smile again
and opens her sketchbook. The page is
filled with black-ink drawings of faces.
All of them wear a different expression.
Some are smiling, some frowning,
some look surprised. I'm no art expert,

but the faces are so realistic, I gasp. "These are fantastic."

"No, they're not. They're just sketches for an exercise I'm working on."

I blink at her. "An exercise?"

"Yeah. I'm trying to capture the details that show what people are feeling." She flips the page over and points out a face that's maybe—sad? "See this? It's terrible. I was trying to get the expression of someone lying."

"Oh."

"It's hard to pinpoint certain facial cues." She sighs heavily. "If I can't master that, I'll never make it as an animator."

I blurt, "Maybe I can help."

"You can?" she asks. "How?"

How? Good question.

From out of nowhere comes this lie. "I've been studying this sort of thing myself. Not for drawing. I suck at drawing. But, see, I plan to be a mentalist. Like those detective guys on TV that read people's faces. They can tell when someone is lying. And they use all those little clues to solve crimes."

"For real?" Ella asks. "You're into that?"

"Oh yeah." I nod. "Totally. I practice all the time."

Behind the glasses, her brown eyes narrow. "Are you just saying that?"

"No. I swear." I can't look at her. I turn and scan the front of the school. Shouldn't the principal be out here to lecture us by now? I need something to save me.

And then the second miracle of the day appears. Standing beside the front steps is the guy who let off the stink bomb. I know it's him because I saw him do it. I was on an errand for my teacher. I'm the sort of guy who gets asked to do those things—trustworthy, reliable me.

Anyway, classes were in session, and the halls were empty. Except for that kid. I don't know his name.

I've seen him around, a scrawny kid with a nasty sneer. He ran by me with a plastic bag, dropped it at the end of the hall and kept going. Seconds later, the bag started spewing. I did what any thinking man would do. I yelled, "Bomb!" and ran. I only paused long enough to pull the fire alarm.

Minutes later, here I was. Beside Ella. Claiming that I plan to be a mentalist. She's still watching me. Maybe she's waiting for me to say more about reading faces.

I point out the scrawny kid. "Look. I'll prove it to you. See that guy? See how he's twitching?" This is true. "And now he's whispering in his buddy's ear?" The scrawny kid and his friend are laughing. "Now he's looking around to see if anyone's watching him." I shift my gaze to Ella. My voice has a ring of authority as I say, "He's got guilt written all over him. He let off the stink bomb."

Sunlight glints off Ella's glasses as she turns from me to the kid and back again. "That's amazing," she whispers. "I think you could be right."

"Perps can't resist watching the mayhem they cause." I may actually sound like I know what I'm talking about.

She stares at the kid. "Sneaky-looking little creep, isn't he?"

"Yeah."

"Do you think you should say something?" She looks around and suddenly raises her arm to point. "There's Principal Garnet." Her gaze tracks back and forth between the principal and scrawny kid.

Principal Garnet studies the crowd from his vantage point on the steps. His glare passes over us and keeps traveling. A moment later, he charges down the steps and takes scrawny kid by the arm. As he's hustled away, scrawny kid sneers and flips us the finger.

Chapter Two

A strange feeling rises up in me when scrawny kid flips us off. I don't know if I've ever felt it before. It's hot and fierce, like jalapeño juice on chapped lips. (I hate that.) But it's mixed with something that makes my chest swell. I'm reminded of those birds on nature shows fluffing up their feathers for battle. I have a weird urge to run after the finger flipper and demand that he apologize. To Ella.

Nobody should be rude around a sensitive girl like Ella. I glance at her to see how she's handling the insult. She's got her sketchbook open in the crook of one arm. And she's drawing. Fast. I've never seen anyone handle a pen so skillfully. Our math teacher, Mr. Jones, has astonishing speed when he writes equations on the blackboard. But Ella makes Mr. Jones look like a slacker.

"Poop," Ella says. Her pen stops.

I can't guess what poop has to do with anything. But I agree with her. "Yeah."

"I really wanted to capture that expression. I'm close, but…" She sighs deeply. "I'd say it was defiance. What do you think, Angus?"

"Um." I think I don't know what she's talking about. I squint at the drawing and am startled to recognize scrawny kid.

And his middle finger. "Holy moly," I say. "That's unbelievable."

Ella shakes her head. "Something is off. I've managed to show his anger, but his defiance isn't there." She studies the sketch. "What did I miss? Something here in the brow line?" She points. "Or in the way his mouth is twisted?"

Uh-oh. Angus the Mentalist should have an opinion about this. Sweat breaks out on my forehead. It slicks over the palms of my hands and the bridge of my nose. My glasses start sliding. If she looks at me now, it will be over between us. Someone with *half* her talent could tell I'm a big fat fraud. Actually, I'm a skinny fraud, but whatever.

"It's the twisted line," I choke as I run away. I disguise the run as a dignified jog. I call another lie over my shoulder. "I think I left a Bunsen burner turned on."

Shahid and I have been friends since we were eight. We met six years ago at science camp. We bonded over a toilet-tissue experiment. We were the only kids who wanted to learn which tissue was the most biodegradable. It wasn't hard, but it required patience to soak the different brands until they fell apart. The next step, putting the samples through a strainer to see which left the most paper undissolved, was more hands-on.

The other kids thought our project was weird. They were more interested in fizzing Alka-Seltzer or watching the gas in yeast blow up balloons. Shahid and I were alone in our belief that the toilet-tissue results were useful. We were able to go home and tell our parents which brand was best for the planet.

Unfortunately, my father then insisted I compare how much bleach was used in the production of each brand and whether they used recycled paper.

He peered over the top of his glasses and said, "Consider all variables, Angus."

Shahid and I followed my dad's advice and became toilet-tissue experts. The main thing we learned was that few people are interested in toilet tissue.

Shahid's father reacted by signing him up for baseball. That was a disaster. Not only were the other players hostile about tissue talk, but Shahid had terrible hand-eye coordination. He never once hit or caught a ball. His father finally stopped making him go, but only on the condition Shahid *never* mention tissue again.

For me, it was my mother who trashed the tissue. She said the most biodegradable brand was no better than using newspaper. She also found it embarrassing. One of her women friends claimed our tissue gave her a paper cut.

None of that matters now except to show that my friendship with Shahid went through many strainers and didn't dissolve. If anything, the trial by tissue gave us a solid kinship.

When I tell him about my encounter with Ella, he stares at me, eyes wide. "You lied to her?" he asks. "The girl who has that strange effect on you? The one whose house you keep making me walk past?"

"I only made you walk by there once," I say.

"Three times. I'm including the times you pretended we had to go that way for exercise." He holds up a hand, palm out, to stop me from speaking. "Here's what we'll do. I'll ask again if my father will adopt you. It's your only hope."

Solid kinship we have. But there are some cultural differences. "I already have a father, Shahid."

"But will he find a wife for you?" he asks.

I glare at him. "How many times do I have to tell you? It doesn't work like that in my family. And just because

14

I *like* someone doesn't mean I'm looking to get *married*."

"Not yet. But one day, when you are a man. And without a father to arrange it for you, I fear your chances are very bad." His shrug is sorrowful. His loose joints make him easy to read. It's got something to do with the way he's put together. Long skinny arms, long legs, long neck, long feet. Even his kneecaps are elongated. He's like a baby giraffe, long-ness all over the place. He moves like that too—all over the place.

But when Shahid makes deliberate gestures, he is very expressive. That gives me an idea. "We're smart, aren't we?"

Shahid grins. "You want to forget this girl and get back to work on Gordon?"

Gordon is the remote control robot we've been building for the past six months. We plan to enter him into a competition this summer. "No. Forget Gordon," I say.

Shahid gasps.

"I don't mean forget him forever. Just for a minute. Or a couple of days. I want us to put our brains to work on something else. I have a plan to fix my problem with Ella. Think about this. How hard can it be to become a mentalist?"

He shakes his head. "A mentalist is a strange person."

"What do you mean?"

"They're supposed to have psychic skills. Have the ability to read minds. You can't become one, just like that." He snaps his fingers. He tries to, anyway. His snaps never make a sound. "Furthermore," he says, "mentalists believe that only our minds are real. Everything else, even physical objects, are here only because we *think* they are."

"Yeah, right," I scoff.

"I'm just telling you what they believe," he says. "I'm not saying I agree."

"How do you know all this?" I ask.

Shahid looks away.

"Shahid?"

"When you went on vacation last summer…" He pauses before muttering, "I decided to become a magician."

I squint at him. "What does that have to do with anything?"

"Some mentalists perform magic acts." Shahid sighs before adding, "That's the part I wanted to try—doing magic."

"You never mentioned this before."

"It was a brief phase. There was a problem with the artificial fog I made in our kitchen. It was very thick. My parents were, you know…" He shrugs. "I had to give it up."

"I see." I watch Shahid for a moment. We're in our lab—the family room in my basement. Without thinking, I pass him a bag of chips. He grabs a handful and stuffs them into his mouth. And suddenly, I have renewed hope.

Chapter Three

I watch Shahid munching and tell him, "You don't like those chips."

He stops chewing, and his eyes widen.

"And your eating them suggests to me that you don't like this conversation. You see? Having food in your mouth is a convenient way to avoid talking about my idea."

Shahid's swallow is loud.

"Come on, Shahid. What's the real problem?"

"I don't think you want to get involved with this girl. Because if you do, then…" He stops.

"Then what?" I ask.

"Then you'll never have time for Gordon," he says.

"*What?*" I snort. "Like that could ever happen. All we have to do is spend a couple of days doing light research on faces. And maybe some fieldwork. We can conduct experiments now."

Shahid frowns. "How?"

"I'll tell you how. Right now, you're frowning. That tells me that you're thinking about something."

"Do you want to know *what* I'm thinking?" he asks.

I squint at him. "Don't tell me. Let me guess." I study his face carefully.

"You're thinking about my idea. And… that's it."

Shahid rolls his eyes. "You can't tell I think you're crazy?"

"Don't kid around. This is serious." An image of Ella's smiling face floats into my mind. "I have to try, Shahid. If I can avoid her for the next few days while I learn how to read people, everything will be fine. I'll be able to talk to her openly. It'll be like I never lied."

"Your logic is faulty," Shahid says. "Unless you've found a way to alter the space-time continuum, the lie has already happened."

Sometimes Shahid can be annoying. "Fine," I say. "The lie happened. But I've liked Ella for eons. Possibly as long as five months. In all that time, I never got up the nerve to talk to her. Now that I finally have, I want to do it again. As my friend, I'd like you to help me."

"Why not just admit your lie? If she's as nice as you say she is, she will forgive you."

I give him a look. "Shahid."

"Fine," he sighs. "I'll help. What do you want me to do?"

I grin. "Excellent. How about this? You make a face, and I'll try to guess what it is."

He stares blankly.

"That's good. That's the face of Missy Turner in math class. It means you don't understand." My grin widens. "See? I can do this. Now, make the face of defiance. I need to know that one."

Shahid's attempt to show defiance is useless. He simply drops his head to the table. It hits with a solid clunk.

"No, no," I tell him. "I need to see your face."

He moans, and when he finally looks up, his face is all scrunched.

He puts a hand to his forehead and moans again.

"I'm pretty sure that's pain," I say. "But that's okay. I should know that one too."

At one time, it would have been easy to avoid Ella at school. Ella sightings were rare. But recently, that's changed. She is no longer as elusive as Shahid's hand-eye coordination. Even though yesterday was the first time I actually spoke to her, she has been popping up almost daily.

Today I see her more often than ever. I narrowly avoid a close encounter in the cafeteria. When I round a corner in the library, she's in the very aisle I had planned to enter. I ask Shahid to go on high alert. This is a system we created long ago to avoid Some People—otherwise known as bullies—when they're in mean mode. Shahid's height makes him an excellent lookout, and he doesn't fail me now. When I attempt to visit my locker at the end of the day, he spots Ella in close range. I dodge her for the third time by ducking into the washroom.

"Phew," I say.

"Exactly," says Shahid. "Maybe we should reconsider studying the ninja arts."

We've discussed this before. Ninjas receive training in stealth. Stealth would be a handy skill. But when we found out we'd also have to learn combat skills, we put that plan on hold. Neither of us is comfortable with violence.

"There's no time for ninja study now," I say. "Faces are my top priority."

A guy we know simply as Grunt emerges from a toilet stall. "Ergh," he grunts. "Freaks. Ungh." And he leaves.

Shahid's eyes widen, and he covers his mouth and nose with a hand. I would call his expression "stricken." He croaks, "Grunt didn't wash his hands."

I nod. "He never does. And you know what? You make that same face, every time. Can you freeze like that for a moment? I'd like to study the details."

Shahid doesn't freeze. He drops his hand, his eyes narrow and a whole bunch of other stuff happens, fast. Little changes in his face occur that involve his brows, his nostrils and his mouth. And then he slaps his hand back in place and tries to fake the face. His eyes go superwide, and something funny happens to his ears. They move.

"Forget it," I say.

"What?" he asks. "This is the face. Go ahead. Study it. Take notes if you want."

"No. It won't work. You're just like an atomic particle, Shahid. You behave differently when you're being watched. I really need to find a mentalist manual."

"Just go online." He sighs. "There's plenty there."

"So you know more about them than you said," I accuse.

"I know it takes years of study."

"I don't have years." I crack the washroom door open and peer out. "But I might have luck. Looks like the coast is clear. Let's go."

We step into the hallway. It's almost empty now. It's amazing how quickly students clear out at the end of the school day. I go to my locker and am dialing in my lock combination when Shahid makes a peculiar sound. "Gack."

"Huh?" I ask.

And a different voice says, "Angus?" It's Ella.

I spin around so fast that I feel dizzy. Or maybe it's seeing her that makes me disoriented. Whatever it is, I gape at her and say nothing.

"I'm so glad I found you," she says.

I shoot a look at Shahid, who is bobbing in the background. He's shifting from foot to foot and shrugging his shoulders. I suspect that means he knows he failed me.

"Ella," I squeak.

And then a very strange thing happens. Ella emits a little whimper and starts blinking rapidly. Her mouth quivers, and she opens her arms wide. For one terrifying second, I think she expects me to hug her. This is exactly what my Nana Carter does when she wants a hug. Not that hugging Ella would be like hugging Nana. But it would take a lot of nerve.

Happily, before I can react, Ella blurts, "It's gone!"

"Gone?" I repeat. "It? Uh…"

"My sketchbook. Someone stole it out of the art room."

"No!" I gasp.

"*Yes*. I just left it for a few minutes, on my work table. And when I got back—" Her voice breaks, and she whimpers again.

"That's terrible," I say. "Did you report it to the teacher?"

"Yeah. But he…I don't know. He just seems to think I lost it. Or that someone picked it up by mistake." Ella sobs as she adds, "But I don't believe that. I did a drawing on the cover of my book so it would be unique."

"Then it should have been obvious that it was yours."

"Exactly." Ella fastens her brown eyes on me. "Angus? Do you think you could use your mentalist skills to help me figure out who took it?"

My mouth opens and closes and opens and closes, and nothing comes out. Finally, a gruntlike sound occurs. And that's it.

Ella drops her gaze to the floor. "That's okay," she mutters. "You don't have to help me." She turns away.

"Wait!" Boldly, I reach for her arm.

I don't actually catch it, but she stops and says, "Yes?"

Shahid is spinning one of his long arms in a circle. It looks like he's trying to turn the handle of a large crank. I have no idea what this means. But then he mouths the words, "Tell her!"

He wants me to tell Ella the truth. I gaze at her standing there waiting for me. She looks like a puppy hoping for a treat. And I blurt, "I'll help you."

Chapter Four

Ella's smile is warm—bright. It's as beautiful as the gaseous outer layers of star
glow. "Thank you, Angus," she breathes.

"No problem," I croak. And once
again, I catch Shahid's movements in
the background. This time he's simply
shaking his head.

"So what do you think we should do
first?" Ella asks.

"Uh..."

There's a space of silence until Shahid says, "Maybe we should visit the scene of the crime."

"Absolutely," I say. "That's definitely first."

"Really?" Ella asks. "But I already searched the art room. It's not there."

"No. Of course not." My mouth feels dry. "But it would be helpful for me to see the, uh, layout of the room." This sounds lame, even to me. And then inspiration strikes. "Also, I'd like you to tell me who was in the room at the time. And where they were positioned."

"Oh." Ella nods. "That makes sense. But I'm not sure I can remember where everyone was."

"That's why we need to go there," I say. "It'll help jog your memory."

"Right." Ella glances down the hall. "Should we go now?"

"No time like the present, I always say. Ha ha." I don't always say that. I never say that.

Shahid rolls his eyes, but Ella just says, "Okay," and starts walking.

I follow, and Shahid falls in beside me. I think he only does this so he can jab his pointy elbow into my ribs. I refuse to look at him. I don't have time for his opinion right now. I *know* I'm an idiot. The question is, how can I prevent Ella discovering it too?

The answer is obvious. I must continue to avoid her. By the time we get to the art room, I've got an updated plan. If it was a computer program, it would be called Avoidance ~ Version 2.0. I barely pay attention when Ella points out the last known location of the sketchbook. That changes when she mentions the girl who shares her worktable.

"She's really good at sculpting in clay. I let her borrow my sketches when she was working on her bust."

Shahid and I make eye contact, and I know he's thinking what I'm thinking. "Um," I begin. "She used your sketches to work on her bust?"

Ella's forehead wrinkles. "Yeah. You know, like one of those?" She points. Sitting on a shelf is one of those disturbing statues of a head, neck and shoulders.

"Oh. Right." I feel my face getting warm. It's possible I may need to learn about art too. I shrug off my back-pack, reach in and fish around for a notebook and pen. When I turn back to Ella, I'm ready to ask, "So what is this girl's name?"

"I don't think she'd steal my book," Ella says.

"Probably not." I hold my pen ready to write. "But she has a motive. We need to consider all potential suspects."

Ella sighs. "I guess. Her name is Rachel. Rachel Stone."

I gape at Ella. I know Rachel Stone. Okay, *know* may be an exaggeration. But I know who she is. *Everyone* knows who she is. "The Gaga Girl."

Behind her glasses, Ella's eyes flash. "People shouldn't be judged by what they wear."

I hold up a hand. "Of course not. No. I just meant…"

"She's got an artistic *soul*," Ella says. "She can't help expressing it."

"Right." I nod.

Shahid emits a sound. "Gack."

"Huh?" I ask.

Then a new voice demands, "What are you people doing in here?"

We turn and see the art teacher, Mr. Wilder. Everyone knows who he is too. He stands with his arms folded across his chest. His long gray hair has partially escaped its ponytail.

The trademark ponytail, bound with beaded leather and feathers, is one of the things that make him stand out. Another is his habit of wearing dresses. Shahid has told me they aren't really dresses, they're caftans or something. They still look like dresses.

His gaze rakes over us, and I notice his eyes are bloodshot. He doesn't look friendly. More like a snake preparing to strike. When his beady eyes find Ella, he raises an eyebrow. "Ella? You know students aren't permitted in here without supervision."

Ella's cheeks flush pink. "Sorry, Mr. Wilder. I forgot my favorite pencil." She raises her hand and waves a pencil.

"Hmph," Mr. Wilder says. There's an edge to his voice as he adds, "Such dedication. Even on a Friday. On your way then. I need to lock up."

We turn as one and leave. Once we're out the door, I mutter, "*Now* he's concerned about security? Seems like a case of too little, too late."

Ella is still pink. "I guess." She takes a deep breath and asks, "So what should we do next?"

Here's where Avoidance ~ Version 2.0 comes in. "I have a few leads to follow," I say. "But while I'm conducting the investigation, it's best if you aren't seen with me."

Ella stops walking and stares. "Why not?"

I talk fast. "If people see us together, as in, if the *culprit* sees me with you, it will tip them off."

Together, Ella and Shahid say, "Huh?"

I force myself to speak slowly and clearly. "Picture this. Let's say I want to check out a suspect like Gaga...I mean, Rachel. I would observe her from a slight distance. I'd watch for clues, such as a glimpse of the sketchbook. Or her

displaying guilty or furtive glances."
This sounds impressive, even to me.

I go on. "If the suspect noticed *me*
lurking nearby, they'd think nothing of
it. But if they saw *you*"—I nod at Ella—
"they'd know we were after them.
Therefore, we must split up at once."

"Oh," Ella says. Her lower lip
quivers in a fascinating way, and she
drops her gaze to the floor. "But..."
She's quiet for a moment, and then asks,
"How will I know what's happening?"
She raises her eyes again. "Can we keep
in touch on Facebook?"

Facebook, she says. I tried that. But
I never got into it. My only "friends"
on there were Shahid and my mother.
It didn't matter before, but it would be
embarrassing if Ella saw how pathetic
I am at social networking. Now that I
think about it, that's a cruel aspect
of Facebook. Why should the number of
"friends" we have be publicly displayed?

I shake my head. "That's too risky," I say. "Suspects could notice our connection there too. How about email?"

She smiles. "Okay. Do you want me to write down my address for you?"

"Sure." I smile too and hand her my notebook. Ella writes her address in *my* notebook. Then she asks me for mine and she writes that down too, at the bottom of the page. She tears off the little strip of paper and tucks it into her pocket.

Chapter Five

Shahid and I spend Friday evening online. We start by researching mentalists. It turns out Shahid was right, they *are* a peculiar bunch. Not that there's anything wrong with peculiar. It's cool that some of them create illusions and do magic and all. But to believe that reality is all in the mind? That's pushing peculiar to the limit.

"What if Ella finds out about this crazy stuff?" I moan. "I never should have told her I'm one of them."

"You shouldn't have told her a lot of things," Shahid replies.

"Yeah, yeah. I don't need to hear about it. I need to learn about facial expressions."

We find some sites with drawings of faces showing emotions like anger, confusion and surprise. I study these, and then I test my skill on a site that shows photos of straight-faced people. A second photo of these people displaying an emotion flashes briefly. The site claims that humans often display "micro expressions" that reveal our true feelings. I'm supposed to identify the emotion shown in the flash photos. I get the answer wrong every time.

"I told you," Shahid says. "It takes years to learn how to read people."

I'm getting tired of him being right.
"So it'll take awhile. But I'll bet I can
at least follow clues." I shake out my
hands, pop a few knuckles, and then
get busy typing in a search for detective skills. Thousands of hits come up.
We spend the next hour hopping from
site to site. A standout piece of advice
says it's important to study your suspects.

"Do we even *have* suspects?"
Shahid asks.

"Absolutely. Gaga Girl and
Mr. Wilder."

Shahid snorts. "As if."

I've already entered a search for
Rachel Stone, but almost nothing
comes up for her. "Maybe if I were her
friend on Facebook," I mutter, "I'd find
something there."

"You have no good reason to
suspect her." Shahid sounds very
certain. He thinks he's right yet again.

"And Mr. Wilder? You don't even have a *bad* reason to make him a suspect."

"Yes, I do. He's got beady eyes. And he had a tone of voice."

"A tone of voice?" Shahid scoffs. "Who doesn't have a tone of voice?"

I don't waste time trying to convince him. The fact is, I may have a hunch. Detectives get hunches all the time, and they don't ignore them. So I type in a search for *Wilder Artist Teacher*. I luck out right away when an image of Mr. Wilder as a young man pops up. He wore a ponytail back then too. Plenty of text comes up on the site with his photo, and we start reading.

Years ago, Mr. Wilder was a promising young artist. He had his paintings on display in art galleries. An old write-up says he could be another Picasso. I'm not sure who that is, but it sounds impressive. Sadly for Mr. Wilder, things didn't turn out that way. Other articles trash his work. One says a flock of pooping peacocks could create finer art. Finally, there's a short blurb that says he's fallen to teaching in a public school.

"What's wrong with that?" Shahid asks.

"Don't ask me."

The blurb goes on to say, *Kel Wilder has given up on himself. His failed attempt to pass off another artist's work as his own is proof of that.*

"Whoa!" I tap the computer screen. "See that? Mr. Wilder took someone else's art."

"It doesn't actually say—"

I don't let Shahid finish. "What if he's done it again? Ella's really good, you know. What if he took her sketchbook and he plans on pretending it's his work?"

"Hmmm. That *would* explain him not bothering to look into its disappearance." He blinks a few times, then says,

"Angus, I think for once—*you* could be right."

We exchange high fives, guzzle energy drinks and eat the rest of our red Twizzlers in celebration of this discovery. In Mr. Wilder, we have our prime suspect.

"Wily Wilder," I murmur.

Shahid nods. "Good one."

"Yeah. But if he's *really* wily…" I pause to choose my next words carefully. "Our investigation must be covert."

"As in, we need to spy on him?" Shahid asks.

"Exactly." So we start researching spy gear. We find many amazingly cool gadgets. There's a remote-control robot with a hidden camera. It's expensive, so we discuss installing a camera on Gordon. We soon rule this out because Gordon is two feet tall and makes a loud whirring sound. People would notice him.

K.L. Denman

The next item that captures our attention is the Gryphon Rocket Wing flight pack.

"An actual rocket pack," Shahid breathes. "Can you imagine? We could spy from the air."

Unfortunately, users of the rocket pack must be launched from an airplane. And it isn't actually available yet. If it was, it would probably cost a lifetime of allowance money.

We agree to get practical after that, set some priorities and figure out what we actually *need*. We decide it's important to get audio and video recordings. We could capture evidence and then go home to review it. We might catch Wily Wilder making a micro expression. If we could freeze that moment, we might even be able to figure out what it means.

But all the gadgets that seem perfect aren't. There's an audio and video camera that looks like a button. It comes with extra look-alike buttons. If you sew them all onto a shirt or jacket, the camera button blends in. No one suspects a thing. Sadly, it costs almost $200, and who knows how to sew on buttons?

There's a camera baseball hat. It's large and puffy and looks like something my grandpa would wear. But it would be easy to operate. All you have to do is switch it on and turn toward the person you want to film. If you put the hat on sideways, you don't even have to look at them.

"We're not allowed to wear hats in school," Shahid says. "And it costs more than the buttons."

He's right. Again.

"There must be something we can afford," I whine.

"How about this?" Shahid points at a camera-carrying Happy Face button. A big bright yellow smiling cartoon-face button.

"Shahid." I speak gently. "What do you think would happen to us if we wore that to school? Take a moment. Imagine the reaction of Some People."

"Ah." Shahid's eyes widen. "It could provoke them, couldn't it?"

"Very likely," I say. "And look at the price."

It's after midnight when we discover a spy supply store within bus range. Spies 4 Real is having a Saturday cash-only sale. They have a limited quantity of rearview sunglasses for the blowout price of $30. These sunglasses are equipped with a tiny mirror inside the frame. Wearers of the glasses can watch the mirror and spy on people behind them. We decide to get up early and bus over so we can be first in line.

Chapter Six

Saturday morning arrives, too bright and too early.

"My eyes hurt," Shahid moans. He rubs them and adds, "If I'd known we'd have to wait around in the sun, I wouldn't have let you keep me up half the night staring at a computer."

We're in a small parking lot, waiting for the Spies 4 Real store to open.

The building, with its gray metal door and gray stuccoed walls, isn't welcoming. We tried peering in through the barred window, but the dark tinted glass wasn't giving up any secrets.

"It shouldn't be much longer," I say. "And just think. When we come back out, you'll be the lucky one wearing sunglasses." We were halfway here before I realized my late-night choice of spy gear wouldn't work for me.

"You're sure your parents won't let you get contact lenses?" Shahid asks.

I nod. I have no intention of asking them. I don't tell Shahid that the mere thought of sticking something in my eye makes me queasy.

A clicking sound comes from the store. I turn to find the lights have been switched on and the Closed sign has been replaced with an Open one. More metallic sounds follow. "They've unlocked the door," I say. "Let's go."

We charge through the door and come to an abrupt stop. The store is eerily silent, and it smells funny. It's a chemical cleaner odor, like bleach, only not. The store is chilly and appears almost empty. An expanse of gray floor stretches before us. Only when I look toward the back of the store do I find glass display cases. A man stands motionless behind the farthest one. He's dressed entirely in black, and he's watching us.

"Hey," I croak.

He blinks. He nods, ever so slightly. And he continues staring. There's no hello or even the standard, "Can I help you?"

I exchange glances with Shahid, and we shuffle toward a side display case. We lean our elbows on the glass and peer in. Spaced at precisely equal distances are a variety of objects. All of them are black. Black binoculars, pens, tiny cameras.

"No sunglasses," Shahid whispers.

"Maybe they're on the other side," I whisper back. I don't know why we're whispering. But there isn't even music playing to cover our voices. I swear I can feel the man's menacing gaze boring into my back.

We shuffle over to the display case on the other side of the store. Still no sunglasses. That leaves only the back case. The one with the creepy watchman.

Shahid murmurs, "Maybe we should forget this. We can just order online."

There is no way I'm going to be scared off so easily. I shake my head and hiss, "We already decided that would take too long." I straighten my shoulders and motion for Shahid to follow me. I start walking toward the back, doing my best to appear confident.

"What are you doing?" Shahid asks.

I answer him from the side of my mouth. "Walking. What does it look like?"

"It looks like…I dunno. Like you've got the runs and you're afraid you won't make it to the can."

The Watchman emits a sound. It's very close to a burp and yet, not a burp. I risk glancing at him directly, but as far as I can tell, nothing has changed. He's still doing his stare.

I turn to Shahid and mouth the words, "Shut up."

Shahid lowers his brows, and mouths, "What?"

I roll my eyes, and mouth, "Forget it."

And the Watchman almost-burps again. Loudly. It's so bizarre that Shahid and I freeze in place. I even freeze my eyeballs. What is with this guy? He reminds me of one of those bull-frogs that make huge sounds without changing their faces. But then more sounds emerge from the Watchman, and it takes a moment for me to realize he's laughing. Laughing! At what? Icy fear grips me as I realize he may be insane. I unlock my eyeballs and slide them toward Shahid. His eyes are goggle-wide. The part of my brain that is still operating realizes that Shahid's face displays terror.

We should run.

"Mwaahaahaa," goes the Watchman. And then he forms words. "You guys. Please tell me you're here for someone else."

"Wha...?" My voice fails. I take a breath and try again. "What do you mean?"

"I mean," he says, "*you're* not planning to spy on anyone, are you?"

"As a matter of fact..." A movement from Shahid makes me pause. Down low at his side, he's waving a hand. Why? Then I understand. He's saying we shouldn't tell the Watchman anything. "As a matter of fact," I repeat, "that's right. We came to pick up some sunglasses for...a friend."

"Is that so?" he asks. "Then step this way. The sunglasses are right here." He raps a knuckle on the case in front of him.

"Oh. Good." I square my shoulders and approach the case. There they are, three whole pairs of them.

"Do you want to try them on?" the Watchman asks. He's still smirking.

"No. No, that's fine." I unzip the pocket on my cargo shorts and pull out my wallet.

"I only have size large in stock," he says.

"That's okay. My, uh, friend has a big head."

"Uh-huh." He shrugs and removes a pair from the case. He rolls them into a sheet of tissue, places them in a bag and says, "That'll be thirty-three dollars and sixty cents."

"Thirty-three sixty? Oh. Right. I guess there's tax." I forgot about tax. I won't have enough money left to take the bus home. I look at Shahid and remember he too had just enough for the bus. Past shakedowns for lunch money have trained us to carry the bare minimum. I peer hopefully into my wallet, but nothing extra has appeared.

"Tell you what," says the Watchman. "Seeing as you're short of cash, if you'll give me your story, I'll forget the tax."

I flinch, then look at him narrowly. "How do you know I'm short of cash? And our *story*? What story?"

"Kid, I couldn't be in this business without knowing a thing or two about reading people. You guys are so obvious." He sighs. "Let's just say I like a good…story. If you want to save yourself the tax, tell me why you want the glasses. What are you planning to do?"

I look at Shahid. He shrugs. Now that the Watchman has started talking, he doesn't seem so bad. And this seems like a clear-cut bargain. So I tell him about Ella's stolen sketchbook and Mr. Wilder.

He doesn't say a word the entire time. When I'm finished, he just stands there with a funny twitch in his throat. Then he reaches under the counter and pulls out a roll of Life Savers candy. He puts them in the bag with the sunglasses and says, "Thanks. That'll be thirty dollars even."

I hand over the money and take the bag. "Uh. Thank you."

"Life Savers?" Shahid mutters.

"I give them to my special customers," the Watchman says. "Good luck, boys."

"Thanks," we say together and leave. As the door closes behind us, we hear him almost-burping again. Loudly.

Chapter Seven

"Maybe we could try duct tape," I say.

"You want to tape them to my head?" Shahid's voice is shrill. "No way."

When the Watchman told us the sunglasses were large, we should have asked *how* large. I don't believe anybody has a head that big. These shades would be oversized on a gorilla. They make Shahid look like an alien.

Or like those magnified pictures of houseflies with their big bulbous eyes. That wouldn't be so bad, but if he makes the slightest movement, the glasses fall off.

"I've got a better idea," Shahid says. "What if *you* wear them over your regular glasses? We could use twist ties to attach the arms together."

We try this, and it works—sort of. The only problem is that the frame of my regular glasses blocks the rear-view mirror on the sunglasses. We make adjustments with the twist ties and lower the sunglasses so the mirror is visible below my frames.

"All right." I give Shahid thumbs-up. "Let's practice."

We start practicing with my mother. She's in the kitchen, talking on the phone. I back up to the doorway, and Shahid stands in front of me. The idea is that I'll watch my mother in the mirror and tell

Shahid what I see. He'll watch her too and confirm that I'm seeing clearly.

"All I can see is the ceiling," I say. "The angle of the mirror is all wrong."

We retreat to our lab downstairs and adjust the twist ties again. This time, we raise the sunglasses so that the mirror sits above my regular frames.

We return to the kitchen doorway and take up our places.

"Now all I can see is the floor," I complain.

"Try lowering your head," Shahid advises. "And raise only your eyes to the mirror."

I try this. "It's a strain on my eyeballs, but I can see her," I tell Shahid.

"Excellent. What is she doing?"

"She's talking on the phone," I report. "And now she's…"

"Angus?" Mom says. "What are you boys up to now? And why are you holding your head like that? Is something wrong with your neck?"

"It's fine, Mom," I mutter. I straighten up to prove this and add, "We were just leaving."

Back in the lab, we're silent for a time. I remove the sunglasses and catch Shahid gazing fondly at Gordon. Gordon doesn't have eyes, but he has a pair of adapted webcams for visuals.

"Maybe after we find Ella's sketch-book," I say, "we can put a reverse gear in Gordon. Then we can put the sunglasses on him so he'll have a rearview mirror."

"You think?" Shahid grins. "That would be sweet."

I nod. "It would. But for now, what if we put a rubber band around your head to hold the sunglasses on?"

The look on his face tells me he's going to refuse. Briefly, I think I *can* read some things.

"You could fluff your hair over the elastic so it wouldn't be obvious," I add.

"*Fluff* my hair?"

"You know what I mean. Comb it over. Whatever. Come on, Shahid. It's only for a day or so. I'm sure the sunglasses will speed up the investigation. Then we can get back to work on Gordon."

"What about Ella?" he asks.

"What about her?"

"She might take…" He stops. He looks again at Gordon and sighs. "Fine. I'll try the elastic." He does, and we are operational.

After Shahid has gone home, I email Ella a link to the site that exposes Mr. Wilder. I try to think of something clever to write as well, but I can't. I simply sign the email *Agent Angus* and press *Send*.

Immediately, I'm sick with regret. Agent Angus? How lame is that? What was I thinking?

Nineteen minutes later—not that I was waiting and checking every minute or so—I receive a reply. My heart literally skips a beat as I see Ella's name in my inbox. My hand trembles as I open the message. She writes:

Hey Agent Angus,
I'm happy 2 hear from u! It's so great that u r helping me. Thank you! But i think u should check out this link to Mr. Wilder's blog.
C u soon!
Ella

I click on the link and read:

Many years ago, I was accused of presenting another artist's work as my own. Rightly so. I did place someone else's painting in a gallery showing of my work. I did it because that artist begged me for this favor. She was young and fragile, and she was afraid to show her work. She feared the harsh comments of the critics. At the same time, she wanted to see if her work would be appreciated by others.

Somehow, our trick was exposed. I made apologies. But since I refused further comment, many leapt to the conclusion that I'd stolen the work. She wanted me to save face and tell the world the truth, but I could not. You see, I was in love with her. I wanted to protect her. Eventually, I convinced her to be my wife. I took up teaching and delighted in spending time with creative young people. With summers free, my wife and I were able to travel North America and paint to our heart's content. We enjoyed twenty blissful years together.

Last fall, my wife passed away peacefully. Her peace came in part because I promised her I would at last

tell the truth. So here I am, keeping that promise. Nothing further need be said.
   Sincerely,
   Kel Wilder

Oh boy, oh boy, oh boy. I feel like a first-class fool. How could I have been so wrong? I was certain that Mr. Wilder was a dirty rotten thief. In less than a day, I'd convinced myself and Shahid of this. I'd gone on to tell the Watchman and he too believed...something. Thinking about the Watchman reminds me of the Life Savers. The remainder of the roll is in my pocket. I pry off a candy and pop it in my mouth. I get lemon, my least favorite flavor.

I deserve lemon. I *am* a lemon. I suck on the Life Saver and try to sort out my thoughts. I need to figure out where I went astray so I don't do it again. It's complicated, because I'm still in

shock over how I misread Mr. Wilder.
I'd built a false reality in my mind
and—whoa! Maybe that's what mentalists mean when they say reality is
in our head?

I call Shahid and tell him I'm a
mentalist.

He groans so loudly, I have to hold
the phone away from my ear. When he
finally stops, I get a chance to explain.
He doesn't respond right away. And
then he says, "So I guess that's it?"

"What do you mean?"

"You're going to tell Ella the truth?"

"Are you kidding?" I ask. "No.
I'm going to find out who stole the
sketchbook."

There's another space of silence
before Shahid speaks. "We're going to
spy on Gaga Girl, aren't we?"

He's right. When isn't he? "I'll have
a plan in place by tomorrow," I say.

Chapter Eight

I may not know Gaga Girl, but I know where she hangs out. I've seen her at the skate park almost every day for the past month. I pass it on my way home from school. She is not a skater. She's more like an accessory to skaters, because she simply stands about and looks decorative.

I'm trying to convince Shahid that she also spends her weekends being decorative. "It stands to reason that she'll be there on a Sunday," I say. "People have habits, also known as patterns of behavior. *Ergo*, if she's at the park after school, why not today too?"

"Okay, okay. We'll go," Shahid says. His grumpy tone tells me he's anything but okay with going.

"Good man." I make *my* tone cheery. "I'll explain the plan in detail when we get there. For now, all you need to know is that you'll be wearing the sunglasses, and I'll be taking notes."

Shahid pesters me for the details all the way to the park. I refuse to tell him more. This isn't really because I don't have more details. It's just that they're unpredictable. I know our objective is to observe Gaga Girl. Then, if our observations show evidence of her guilt, we may have to interrogate her. I think that detail may worry Shahid. It's best if I get him to the park first, then see what happens next.

I tell him that we'll approach the skate bowl from the west so we can take cover in the clump of trees on that side. All goes very well. We enter the shrubbery and edge forward until we're almost through. I call a halt while we're still concealed by low-hanging branches.

"Wait here," I hiss. "I'm going to see if I can spot her."

"You don't need to whisper," Shahid says. "Nobody will hear us."

He has a point. It's a sunny afternoon, and the skaters are out in full force. The wheels on their boards rumble on the concrete surface and clatter on pipes. Music pumps from a stereo.

I shrug and then shuffle over to a tree trunk. I hold on to it while craning my head until I have a clear view. I almost lose my grip on the tree when I spot our target.

"There she is!"

"No duh," Shahid says. "I can see her from here."

The fact is, Rachel Stone is rather hard to miss. She got her nickname last year when she began dressing like (one assumes) her idol. Today is no exception. I decide to let go of the tree trunk and make notes.

Suspect: Rachel Stone, alias Gaga Girl
Description: Girl disguised as rainbow
Height: Taller than me/shorter than Shahid
Hair Color: Purple
Distinguishing Features: Blue wing-style mask with curly tendrils protruding from tips. Shiny green cape, knee length. Brilliant yellow micro dress. Orange legs (difficult to tell if legs are painted or if she is wearing stockings). Red ankle boots.

This is what I mean about her being decorative. Most days she's satisfied with looking like she's ready to go on stage. Days like today, when there's an apparent theme, must take a lot of planning. Previous costumes have made her appear as a plant, a cloud and a rock.

"What is she doing?" Shahid asks. "Is that a sketchbook?"

"Huh?" I look up from my notes, and, sure enough, Rachel is holding something. Now it's time for my plan to go into action. "Okay! Here's what I want you to do, Shahid. See that low wall over there? The one just beyond where Rachel is standing?"

"Yeah."

"I want you to put the glasses on and walk over there. Walk casual-like, as if you're just sort of wandering."

"Wandering?" Shahid echoes.

"You know what I mean. Don't draw attention to yourself. Once you're there,

I want you to keep your back to Rachel. Maybe lean your elbows on the wall and make it appear that you're gazing out the other way, bird-watching or something. But make sure you can see her in the mirror. Got it?"

He stares at me.

"Okay," I sigh. "I'll go over it again. I want you to walk casually over to—"

"I get it!" he snaps. "What are you going to be doing while I'm *bird*-watching?"

"I'm going to go off that way." I point toward the street. "Beyond the wall. Then I'll circle back and crouch down on the other side, close to you. You can tell me what you see, and I'll take notes."

"Oh, man," Shahid moans. "Why can't we just walk by her and get a closer look at the book?"

"Because," I say. "That's too…"

"Easy?" he cuts in.

"No. It's too obvious. What if we can't get a good look at it? We can't keep walking back and forth until we do."

"Fine," he says in a tone that tells me it's not fine. He pulls the sunglasses out of his backpack. He opens them and stretches the elastic over his head. He sets the glasses in place, and there's an audible *snap* when he releases the elastic. "Ow!"

"Don't forget to fluff your hair," I tell him.

"Right," he mumbles. "Fluff my hair." He's still mumbling as he stomps away.

"Casual, Shahid," I call after him. "Wandering."

He surprises me by responding with a rude gesture. That's totally not like him. It reminds me of something, but I can't remember what. I decide it's not important and set off on my own route to the wall.

Chapter Nine

What appeared to be a low wall from the skater side is a high wall from the other side. It's one of those concrete-block retaining walls that separates the ground into two levels. The lower level is the flat surface of a soccer field. It's perfect. I can glimpse Shahid's head above me as I take up my position.

"Shahid," I hiss. "Can you hear me?"

"Yesss," he hisses back.

"Can you see Rachel in the mirror?"

"Yesss."

I'm so delighted, I could dance a jig. Not that I dance jigs, but if I did, I would.

"Excellent. What is she doing?"

"I don't know."

"What does it *look* like she's doing?" I ask.

He whispers, "It looks like she's staring at my back."

"What?"

"I *said*," he says, "she's staring at me."

This is worrisome. "Has she been doing that the whole time?"

"No. Before this, she was unpacking art supplies. Paint and stuff." There's a pause before he adds, "And also looking at the sketchbook."

I'm delighted again. "Did you see what was in it? Were there drawings of faces?"

"I couldn't tell. There were drawings, but…" He stops. And then he says,
"Gack."

"Huh?"

And a girl's voice says, "Excuse me.
I was wondering—how long do you
think you'll be here?"

"Uh," Shahid stammers. "I can't say
for sure. But going by statistics, I'll be
around for another seventy years."

There's a gap in the conversation,
and then the girl laughs. "Very funny.
I meant, how long will you be standing
in front of this wall?"

"Oh. I don't know. I hadn't thought
about it." Even from a distance, I can
hear Shahid swallow. "It's not something I generally do."

Another space of silence follows.
Then the girl asks, "You don't generally stand in front of walls, or you don't
generally think?"

"Walls," Shahid blurts. "That's what I meant. Thinking, I do all the time."

This seems like the right answer to me, but the girl sounds disappointed. "Oh. That's too bad. I find thinking interferes with life."

"Really?" Shahid squeaks.

"Yeah. Thinking gets in the way of the pure experience, you know? The mind can be such a fake place."

"Fake? But…but," Shahid stammers. "Oh. Huh. I guess that would make you the opposite of a mentalist."

"What did you say?" she asks.

"I don't know." Poor Shahid. He's not himself.

"That word," she mutters. "*Mentalist.* It rings a bell. Oh!" And suddenly, there she is—Rachel. She's leaning over the wall, looking straight down at me. Beneath the violet hair and the blue mask, her mouth is smiling. "You must be Angus." She turns to Shahid. "And you're his friend, right? Ella told me to watch for you."

I'm stupefied. This makes no sense at all. I can't speak, but that's okay because Rachel keeps going. "She didn't tell me you two were so...cute. And artsy."

"Artsy?" Shahid's voice is faint.

Rachel nods. "Definitely artsy. I've never seen shades like yours. They make such a *large* statement."

"They do?" Now Shahid sounds really confused. "What are they saying?"

She giggles. "You tell me."

"I can't," he says. I know that Shahid means this literally.

It's time for me to step up and save him. I try out my voice, and it works. "Ella told you about us?"

"For sure," Rachel says. "She told me you're a—what was the word again? A mentalist. And that you're helping her find her sketchbook. She said you'd be checking around."

I can't believe this. Ella needs more help than I thought. Tipping off the suspects is so...naïve. "Yeah, well," I mutter. "I guess you know how important Ella's drawings are to her."

"They're very important," Rachel says. "She's really good. Way better than me. You should see how pathetic mine are."

Aha. She may think by offering to show me her art, *I'll* think she must not have anything to hide. But I can't be thrown off so easily. I tell her, "I doubt your drawings are pathetic. I'd be happy to see them."

"Really? Then come on up here and I'll show you." She disappears from view.

I whisper to Shahid, "Are you okay?"

"No," he says. "No, I'm not."

"I'll be right there," I tell him.

I don't have to go far to find my way around the retaining wall. I hike up a little slope and march toward Rachel. Scattered on the ground at her feet are felt pens, spray-paint cans and a sketchbook. She picks up the sketchbook and holds it aloft as I approach. Once I'm there, she flips it open.

"See? These are my graffiti ideas."

The drawings are almost as bad as something I'd do. They're nothing more than rough, blocky shapes. "Huh," I mutter. "Graffiti ideas?"

"Yeah." She points at the retaining wall. "That one is mine. The park people are letting us do our own thing around here."

"Oh."

"Cool," Shahid croaks. "I guess that's why you were wondering how long I'd be standing in your way."

"You got it. But hey, no worries. I'm glad I got to meet you two."

I mutter, "Likewise."

"Maybe you'll come back sometime and see how it turns out?" she asks. She's looking at Shahid.

"Yes," Shahid answers solemnly, like he's making a promise. "I will."

"Good. Are you guys done with the wall?"

We nod.

"Then I'm going for it." With a grand gesture, she tosses back her green cape.

Shahid and I mutter, "Good luck."

We're almost home when Shahid says, "Her legs were painted orange." His tone is one of wonder.

Chapter Ten

Usually, the minute my heads hits the pillow, I fall asleep. Not tonight. No, I lie awake thinking about Shahid telling me that I must admit to Ella that I'm not a mentalist. I can't read facial expressions. I have no idea who stole her sketchbook.

I know Shahid is right. By lying to Ella to get her to like me, I'm no better than a player. I decide that I'm not actually a player, because I think those guys lie to lots of girls. Still, I am a liar.

I try to picture telling Ella "The Truth." What words could I use? Would she be angry? Would she never speak to me again? My mind shies away from this awful scene. I switch to picturing the way she looked at me like a hopeful puppy. I recall her skill with a pen and the amazing likeness she drew of the scrawny kid.

This leads me to remember the stench of the stink bomb and the scrawny kid flipping us off. What a jerk.

Wait a minute. Was he looking straight at us when he did that? Wasn't Ella's arm raised, pointing toward Principal Garnet? She was pointing at something. I was a bit distracted when all that happened. Or would that be disoriented? Whatever it was, I know I was affected by Ella's presence.

And then an idea strikes me with such force that I sit bolt upright in bed.

Scrawny kid stole Ella's sketchbook! Of course he did. He thinks she ratted him out to the principal. He took her book for revenge.

Wow. This is it. I know it. It makes complete and total sense. Once again, I picture scrawny kid flipping us the finger. I remember Shahid doing that very thing to me today. At the time it reminded me of something. It's as if my brain knew more than me. Is that possible? It's my brain. It shouldn't know things that I don't know. Although in all fairness, my brain did try to get in touch with me.

None of that matters now. The important thing is that I know who stole Ella's sketchbook! This feels so good I decide I can reply to her email. I get up and send this message:

FYI: Update on investigation. Have identified the culprit. Have large hope that recovery of your sketchbook will happen soon.

Agent Angus

PS Thanx for the link to Mr. Wilder's blog. Am very sorry about his wife.

Now all I have to do is figure out how to get the book back from Scrawny.

"The first thing we have to do," I tell Shahid, "is find him." We're standing at the top of the stairs overlooking the main hall at school. It's one of the best places to observe students.

Shahid shakes his head. "If this kid got caught for stink-bombing, wouldn't he be suspended?"

He has a point, an inconvenient point. "We'll have to find out about that," I say.

"How?" Shahid asks. "We don't even know his name. We can't go into the office and ask the principal what happened to Scrawny."

"Obviously not," I snap. "But the secretary likes me." The warning bell sounds for first class. "If I get sent to the office on an errand today, I'll see what I can find out."

I don't get sent to the office in first period. Nor am I asked to fetch or carry anything for the teacher in second class. I find this frustrating, but by lunchtime I have a new plan. I explain it to Shahid at my locker.

"Who do we know," I ask, "that must overhear many conversations?"

Shahid shrugs. "You tell me."

"Grunt! He's always in the washroom, right? He must hear plenty. He might not have heard Scrawny talking about his bomb plot, but he could have heard something. Like the *name* of the person who set off the bomb."

"Maybe so," Shahid says, "but that doesn't mean he'll tell us. He doesn't like us, for one thing. And for another, he can barely form words."

"I know that. But I have an idea. Let's see if he's there, If he is, follow my lead, okay?"

Shahid heaves a weary sigh and nods.

We proceed to the washroom, and, sure enough, the door to Grunt's cubicle is closed. A quick peek under the door confirms that his feet are there. I turn the tap on and raise my voice. "That was quite the prank." I look at Shahid expectantly.

Shahid frowns and mutters, "Yeah."

"What?" I say loudly.

"I said, yeah." Shahid has caught on and increased his volume.

I grin at him and yell, "I wonder what he put in that stink bomb."

Shahid yells back, "Whatever it was, it sure was smelly."

"Too bad," and then I lower my voice and deliberately garble the next word, "Jasackolon," and I return to yelling, "Got caught."

"No kidding," Shahid shouts. Then he makes his fake name quiet too. "Roboley," he turns up the volume, "thought he'd get away with it."

The toilet flushes and we hold our breath. Grunt emerges. He squints at us and says, "Ergh. You guys. Hah. That idjit Rolf deserved to get caught. Nyuh." And he leaves.

Shahid doesn't display his usual stricken face. He simply casts a sad look at the soap dispenser and sighs. "Did he say Rolf?" he asks.

"That's what I heard," I reply. "The question now is, is Rolf his actual name? Or is that a Grunt-ism?"

"Hard to say."

"Yeah." I ponder deeply for a moment, and then snap my fingers.

"I saw Scrawny talking to someone that day, just before he got nabbed by Principal Garnet. If we could ask that guy if he knows a Rolf...but then we'd have to find *him* too."

Shahid emits another weary sigh. If he keeps that up, I may have to mention that it's not a pleasant habit.

But I ignore that for now because my brain is doing that thing again. It knows something that it's not telling me. I concentrate fiercely. I picture Scrawny Rolf outside the school on stink-bomb day. I see him and then, very clearly, I see his friend. "Aha!" I grin at Shahid. "I know where to find them. Do you remember those guys that always hang around the corner store?"

Shahid's eyes widen. "Those guys?"

I nod triumphantly. "You got it. We'll go there after school."

Chapter Eleven

Our quarry is in sight. Scrawny Rolf and his sidekick are leaning against the brick wall at the corner store, sucking back slushies. Shahid and I have taken up position across the street. We're lurking behind a mailbox.

"Now what?" Shahid asks.

"Well," I say, "we continue to observe."

"You don't know what to do, do you?"

He's right. I don't know what we should do. Part of me wants to march over there and demand that Scrawny Rolf hand over Ella's sketchbook. But clearly, he doesn't have the sketchbook on him. He's so skinny, if he held the book to his chest it would stick out on either side of his rib cage. The surprising fact is, I'm bigger than him.

The same can't be said about his buddy. That guy isn't much taller than me, but he's as wide and solid as a bulldog.

"Angus?" Shahid asks. "What do you want to do?"

"I'm thinking," I say. "On the one hand, we could go over there and interrogate him right now. Or we could wait until they split up." I realize I like my second idea very much. "They're bound to go home sooner or later. And when they do, we'll follow Rolf."

"And then what?"

"Jeez, Shahid. What do you think?" I ask.

Shahid emits his weary sigh.

"If you don't stop that," I say, "I'm going to get very annoyed."

"Stop what?"

"All that sighing. It's getting on my nerves. You sound like an old man who's…I don't know. Tired of the world."

He says, "I don't know what you're talking about."

"Forget it," I mutter. "Look, all we have to do is follow Rolf. If he's still got the sketchbook, he probably stashed it at home. So we'll have to go there to get it anyway."

"What do you mean, 'if he's still got it'? Why wouldn't he have it?"

I answer in a somber tone. "We have to be prepared for the possibility that he destroyed it."

"Oh," Shahid says. "That would suck for Ella."

"It would." I glare across the street at Scrawny Rolf. "He'd better not— Look! They're leaving."

"Yeah," Shahid hisses. "And they're coming straight for us."

My first impulse is to duck behind the mailbox. That's a bad idea. The mailbox isn't big enough to hide us. "Start walking," I urge. "Now."

And so it goes for a time, with Scrawny Rolf and his buddy following us.

"Put on the sunglasses," I tell Shahid.

"I don't have them."

"*What?*" I don't wait for him to answer. "You forget them now, when we could really use them? We'd be able to maintain a proper distance. Keep an eye on them. Observe when they change direction. All that, without ever looking over our shoulders."

"How was I supposed to know this was going to happen?" he asks. "There was no point in bringing them to school. If I put them on there, a teacher would confiscate them."

I emit a Shahid-worthy sigh. "Never mind. Here's what we'll do. We'll take turns looking sideways and use our peripheral vision to see what they're doing. I'll go first." I whip my head over to the right and pretend I'm looking at something across the street. Then I whip my head back into the forward position.

"So?" Shahid asks.

"I think I may have given myself whiplash," I say.

"Casual," Shahid chides. "Wandering."

I refuse to respond.

"Fine," he says. "Be like that. *I'll* look."

From the corner of my eye, I see him ease his head to the side. It's quite impressive. Anyone observing him would believe he was simply gazing at the hedge we're passing by. His pace suddenly slows.

"What are you doing?" I ask.

"They're gone." He comes to a complete halt and turns fully around. "I can't see them anywhere."

"No way." I turn too and scan the sidewalk behind us. He's right. Our quarry has vanished. "That's impossible. Where could they go?"

"We passed an alley back there."

"Oh. Really? Well, okay then. Good stuff. Now we can go back and follow them." We retrace our steps until we come to the mouth of the alley. There, we pause at a solid fence bordering the sidewalk. "This is a blind corner," I whisper. "We shouldn't enter the alley until we know how far down they've gone."

"They can't have got too far ahead," Shahid whispers back. "But they couldn't be too close anymore either."

"Sounds perfect," I say.

But both of us are reluctant to move. And it's a good thing we don't. Very likely, some instinct warned us to maintain our position, because the fence suddenly wobbles. At the same time, we hear the squeak of hinges and a gruff voice calls, "Later, Rolf."

Rolf replies, "Yeah."

And then the alley gate slams shut and the fence goes into a major wobble.

We wait, listening for Rolf's footfalls. Will he come back this way or proceed down the alley? When it's obvious that the crunching sound of feet on gravel is fading, Shahid and I finally exhale.

"Phew," I breathe. And then I realize that this is exactly what I'd hoped for. I motion Shahid forward. "Let's go."

"He'll notice us following him in the alley," says Shahid.

"So?" I feel brave and reckless. "There are two of us and only one of him. And we're bigger. Let's go get

Ella's sketchbook." With that, I step boldly into the alley.

I see Rolf at once. He's only made it past the next yard down. He's shuffling along, hands in pockets, narrow shoulders hunched. I decide it's best to put a bit more distance between us and his large buddy, so I don't call out to him. Instead, I match my pace to his and keep following.

It takes me a moment to realize Shahid isn't with me. I turn to find him still peeping from behind the fence. I jog back. "What are you doing?"

He shakes his head. "I am not the gangsta type, Angus."

I blink a few times before I answer. "And you're telling me this because?"

"Because I have no intention of ganging up on Scrawny Rolf."

I find I need to blink some more before I can answer. "Shahid. You know me better than that. Did you honestly think I plan to hurt him? All I meant about us being bigger is that it seems unlikely he could hurt us."

"Oh. Okay. We better get going then. It looks like he's in a hurry."

"What?" I turn, and sure enough, Scrawny Rolf has picked up his pace. "He must have noticed us! Come *on*!" I launch into a run. This time, Shahid gallops beside me, arms flapping wildly.

Chapter Twelve

I don't do a lot of running. It's surprisingly tiring. But determination must count for something, because we gain on Rolf. When I judge that we're close enough, I slow to a fast walk.

"Hey, you. Rolf." I pause to draw breath.

He turns around and squints at us. "Yeah?"

"I want to talk to you," I say.

"Yeah?" he says again. His squint intensifies. "Do I know you?"

"No," I reply. "You do not. But I believe I know you."

He removes his hands from his pockets. "Izzat right?"

"Yes, indeed." I puff out my chest. "And I believe that you've done a terrible thing."

His brows form a knot. "What are you talking about?"

"I am talking about Ella Eckles's sketchbook." I glare fiercely. "You took it. And I'm here to get it back."

"Ella...what?" The knot on his brow deepens. "Wait a minute. You're not calling me a *thief*, are you?"

I maintain my glare. "Yes. That's exactly what I'm doing. And I'd prefer that you don't play dumb with me."

It's possible that, like my brain, other parts of my body know things that

I don't. I certainly don't tell myself to dodge sideways. But I dodge just in time to avoid Rolf's swing. Then, as if it has a mind of its own, my arm takes a swing at him. It misses by quite a lot, but I don't have time to worry about that, because here comes another jab from Rolf.

I manage to avoid that one too. Then my other arm gets in on the action. It swings way up, and on the way down it almost connects with Rolf's fist. Suddenly, both of my arms are whirling like the rotor blades on a helicopter. Not exactly like that, because my circles are vertical whereas a helicopter's are horizontal. But the action is similar.

As near as I can tell, Rolf's arms are doing the same thing. It's terribly shocking. I'm forced to close my eyes. Occasionally our fists bounce off each other, and it really hurts. I'm becoming exhausted, but have no idea how to make it stop.

And then a voice roars, "Enough!" I feel a pressure on my forehead. My arms drop to my sides like dead things, and I crack open my eyes.

Shahid stands between us with one hand pressed against my forehead and the other against Rolf's. His giraffe arms force us farther apart as he asks, "Do you two have any idea how stupid you look?"

My brain refuses to picture it.

Rolf croaks, "Please don't tell anyone."

"Especially not Ella," I say.

"Who," Rolf demands, "is this Ella?"

"Hah," I say. It's impossible to form a fierce glare with Shahid's hand pressed to my face, but I try. "She's the girl you think ratted you out. So you stole her sketchbook for revenge."

"Say what?" Rolf rolls one eyeball up toward Shahid. "Is this little dude crazy?"

"I'm bigger than you," I tell him. "Did you or did you not set off the stink bomb in school last week?"

Rolf shrugs. "Yeah. So?"

"Did you or did you not get caught by Principal Garnet?" I wriggle to increase my glare power and add, "Shahid, would you kindly remove your hand?"

"Are you going to start flailing again?"

Together, Rolf and I say, "No."

"Fine." Shahid's tone is grudging. "All you have to do is back away."

I can't believe I didn't realize that. I back beyond Shahid's reach and give my head a shake. I look over to see Rolf doing the same thing. For some reason, this annoys me. "Well?" I ask him. "Principal Garnet caught you, right?"

"Yeah, yeah. But I'm pretty sure it was that troll in the can who told him."

The troll in the can. I ponder that for a moment before asking, "And you think I'm crazy?"

He rolls his eyes. "You know who I mean. Everyone knows about the guy in the stall. He practically lives there."

I suddenly get it. "You mean Grunt?"

Rolf shrugs. "I don't know his name. But he's always in there, listening to other people's business." He wrinkles his nose. "And he never washes his hands."

"I know," Shahid moans. "It's so disgusting."

"Too right," Rolf nods. "But whatever. I haven't been at school since the bomb. Garnet suspended me for a week."

I stare at Rolf for a moment. Then I find I can't look at him. He's telling the truth. I know he is. That means he couldn't have been in the art room the next day. He didn't steal anything. My mouth feels dry. I swallow.

"Rolf," I mutter. "I owe you an apology. I thought—but I guess that was all in my head. Never mind. The point is,

I don't think you're a thief anymore. I'm really sorry."

He shrugs his thin shoulders. "Whatever, man. Sounds like you were trying to stick up for a friend. That's cool."

"Really?" I try for a smile. "Thanks. That's very gracious of you."

The knot forms on Rolf's brow again. He looks from me to Shahid and he raises a finger. It's his index finger this time, and he points it at us. "Here's the deal. No one hears about this. We don't talk about it ever. Especially not in the can. Okay? We all square?"

"Absolutely," I say. "Square as square can be. Square as my mother's squares. Like her brownies. I swear, she must measure them before she cuts and—"

"I *got* it," Rolf says. "I've gotta go. I'm late for my paper route." And he runs away.

Shahid looks at me until I finally look back.

"Now," he says. "Now will you tell Ella the truth?"

Chapter Thirteen

There is no doubt that I have to tell Ella who I really am. Or rather, I have to tell her who I'm not. The only part I have to figure out is how. I'm so disturbed by this I can barely eat dinner.

"You need to get more exercise, Angus," Mom says. "Then you'll have an appetite."

Exercise, she says. I got plenty of exercise today. I don't tell her about that. I simply nod and return to worrying.

By early evening, I decide that my best option is to send Ella an email. That seems cowardly, but since it's been our contact method, it makes sense. I log into my email with the idea that I'll compose my message very carefully. I expect it will be as challenging as writing an essay about something mysterious like poetry.

It's startling when my email shows two new messages from Ella. I open the first to find she replied to the one I sent yesterday. The one where I bragged about knowing who the culprit is. She wrote:

Hey Angus,
U r amazing! You already know who took my book? Wow! Can you give me any hints?
With admiration,
Ella

My stomach starts doing gymnastics. I don't know the proper names for all the moves it's making, and I don't care. She thinks I'm amazing? She admires me? Oh boy, oh boy, oh boy.

Oh, girl. You have been misled. That's what I should write to her. I should click the Reply button and type those very words. But I can't. I can only sit and stare at the wonderful words she wrote to me.

Eventually, I rouse from my stupor, draw a deep breath and open her second message.

Angus, u won't believe this! The culprit sent me an email! All it said was, Catch me if you can. *And then below that, there was a photo of one of my drawings. I'm including the picture here in case it has some clues for u. I hope this helps u figure it out.*

Ella

My hand shakes as I scroll down
and find the picture. It's an incredible
drawing of an animated robot. It's so
fantastic, it almost brings tears to my
eyes. And someone stole this from
Ella! What sort of sadistic creep would
do such a thing?

I'd give almost anything to figure
that out. But the only things I've
figured out are that I'm the crummiest
person-reader on the planet, and I'm
clueless about clues. I wouldn't recognize a clue if it jumped up and down
and yelled, "Hey! I'm a clue!"

I gaze at her beautiful drawing and
realize that at least I can save this.
I right-click on it and run my eye down
the list of items in the pop-up box. I'm
looking for *Save* until I notice the item
at the bottom of the list: *Properties*.

Is it possible? Could the thief actually have been dumb enough to leave
the properties attached to the photo?

There's only one way to find out. I open the properties box, and there's the date the picture was taken. Today. Then I slide the cursor over to the Details tab and...

It's all there. I see the number of pixels and the brand of smart phone used to take the picture. The GPS coordinates pinpoint where the picture was taken. I swipe the cursor over the GPS numbers for longitude and latitude and copy them. I paste them into an online street map program. In less than a minute, I'm looking at the street view of the house where the photo was taken.

And I recognize that house. It's Ella's.

Chapter Fourteen

The picture was taken at Ella's house? What does this mean? My brain seizes for a moment. This does not compute. But then my brain starts up again, and my body freezes. Goose bumps spring up willy-nilly, all over my skin. I can't breathe. And then I can breathe, and I'm almost hyperventilating.

Because if this picture was taken at Ella's house, then she's in danger. Big-time. The creepy, sadistic thief sent it to her from her very yard. Or worse yet, from within her home.

I leap to my feet. Then I fall back into my chair and type a frantic reply to her email. *Leave house at once!!!!!!!!!!!*

I scrabble my fingers over the keyboard to bring up a telephone directory. I find the Eckles, but there's no number listed. Once again I leap to my feet, and this time I order them to run.

And run. I run out my back door, around the house and down the street. I make a sharp turn at the corner and run down the next street. I round the final corner that takes me onto Ella's street and I keep running all the way to her front yard.

At that point, I collapse under a shrub. This is okay, because even though it's possible I'll puke, I can still use my eyes to scan the area. I may be crumpled on my hands and knees, gasping for air, but I remain on high alert.

Eventually my breathing returns to something like normal. I see no sign of a stalker, psycho or thief. Not that this is a good thing. In fact, it's bad, because it means the lunatic may be inside the house. I manage to stand, even though my legs feel strangely bendy. I try them out for walking, and they work—more or less. I wobble to the front door and ring the bell.

Footsteps approach from the inside, and then the door swings open to reveal Ella.

"Angus!" she says. Her face turns a rosy shade of pink. "You're here."

"Yes," I say. I lean toward her and lower my voice. "Don't panic. I want you to gather your family and get them out of the house. And then we'll call the police."

Ella's eyes dart about. She licks her lips. Clearly, she's frightened. She tucks a loose strand of hair back behind her ear. "Uh," she says. "Why?"

"Because," I hiss, "I think the guy who stole your sketchbook may be in your house."

Her brown eyes widen. Her mouth forms a circle. The pinkness of her skin deepens, especially on the tip of her nose. And then she starts giggling. She claps a hand over her mouth to stop the nervous giggles, but seconds later, they burst through.

"Ella!" I attempt to sound stern. "You must remain calm. Please, go and get your—"

"Angus," she cuts in. "It was me. *I* took the picture."

"You?" I squeak out the word. "What? No. You *drew* the picture, but…"

"Shhh." She reaches out and places her hand on my mouth. It's as if she found my Off switch. Or maybe it's more like she zapped me with a stun gun. I start tingling all over, and I can't speak.

Ella looks over her shoulder into the house and calls, "I'm going out on the porch." And then she closes the door behind her and points toward a bench. "Can we sit down for a minute?"

I nod. I sit. Ella sits on the opposite end of the bench. She looks down at her shoe toeing the bench leg and then says, "I have a confession to make."

And does she ever. It turns out her sketchbook was never stolen. She made the whole thing up so that she could spend time with me.

"Seriously?" I ask.

She bites her lower lip and nods. "I'm really sorry. It's just that I *like* you, Angus. And I thought you might like me too. I tried for months to get a chance to talk to you. But every time I saw you, you were going the other way. When I finally did

talk to you, that day the school got evacuated? I thought it went well. But then
you had to take off and…" She shrugs.

I'm speechless. All I can do is stare
at her.

Ella's lower lip quivers in that fascinating way. "I don't know what got
into me. But when you said you were
a mentalist and you wanted to solve
crimes, I got this crazy idea." She finally
looks straight at me. "I'm sorry I lied to
you. You probably despise liars."

I emit a sound. "Gack."

"Pardon me?"

I look down at my foot toeing the
bench leg. I have an impulse to run
away, but I've had enough running—in
more ways than one. It's time to confess.
I start with, "Erm." I progress to, "Uh,"
and finish in a rush. "I'm a liar too."

Ella asks, "What do you mean?"

"I mean I'm no mentalist. I can't
read people. I don't have a clue what

people are thinking. I don't even know what *I'm* thinking sometimes."

Ella is quiet, and I risk a quick glance to see how she's taking this. Her head is tilted to one side and, strangely enough, she's wearing that little smile. "Go on," she says.

I find this encouraging. I draw a deep breath and basically barf up my next words. "I lied. I was trying to impress you because I like you too. It seemed like a good idea at the time, but it wasn't."

There. I did it. I told the truth. I don't dare look at her now.

"That's so sweet," Ella says.

I gape at her. "It is?"

"Yeah. Not the lying, of course." She shrugs and smiles bigger. "But... you like me too?"

I nod.

And then her smile fades. "But there's something I don't understand."

Uh-oh. I swallow and ask, "What?"

"You identified the stink bomber. I mean, that was totally impressive, the way you picked him out of the crowd."

I suddenly feel short of breath. I grab at the collar of my T-shirt and tug, but it doesn't help. "Oh," I choke. "That. Ha ha. Funny thing, you see. I see—I mean, I saw—him do it."

Behind her glasses, Ella's brown eyes narrow. "Reeaaally?" The way she draws the word out must indicate something. The question is, what?

I simply nod again.

And she keeps watching me, as if she's waiting for more.

There isn't any more. At least, not any more lies. Should I tell her that? I think I should. "That's it," I say.

"That's it?" she echoes. And her eyebrows go up.

I tug at my collar again. Something about this isn't going well. What am

I missing here? "I wish I'd never done that," I mutter aloud. "I'm really sorry."

Her smile breaks out again, the one that reminds me of the gaseous outer layers of star glow. "Oh, Angus," says Ella. "Me too. Do you think we can just forget all these silly glitches and start over?"

I blink at her. "You mean like a hominid version of a reboot?"

She blinks back. "Yeah. I guess I do mean that."

Shahid's mouth hangs slightly open. We're in our lab, and he's looking over the sketches Ella drew of Gordon. Not Gordon as he is, but the Gordon we always dreamed he could be.

"Amazing," Shahid says. "Who'd have thought a frivolous thing like art could be so useful?"

"Not me," I reply. "But, Shahid? Don't say that in front of Ella, okay?"

Shahid squints at me. "What do you mean?"

"Don't you remember what happened the time I said art was a great hobby?"

His eyes widen. "Oh yeah. Didn't that set off her speech about art being essential for the soul?"

"I think so," I say. "Or was that when she told us life imitates art?"

"Maybe. Did you understand that Ella-ism?" Shahid asks.

I shake my head. "Ella-isms are challenging. Some of them remind me of the mentalists."

"In what way?" he asks.

"You know," I shrug. "All that stuff about reality being what we think it is."

We're silent for a moment, considering this. Finally, Shahid sighs and says, "Thinking about that makes me dizzy."

"Yeah. Me too." Luckily, talking about mentalists has reminded me of a more entertaining time from the past.

"Hey, do you remember when you muscled in between me and Rolf? When we were fighting?"

The stories of our spy days have been retold between us many times. Shahid no longer corrects me when I describe my activity with Rolf as fighting. Already the details are shifting. Some part of my brain knows this, but it doesn't seem to mind.

"I remember," Shahid says. He flexes one of his skinny arms, and sure enough, there's a hint of the bicep he's been building. Then he places the drawing of Gordon in front of me. "And I'm glad you haven't forgotten Gordon."

Maybe Shahid is one person I can read. I know he was worried about me ignoring more than Gordon. Life isn't quite the same with Ella around. My friendship with Shahid was put through another strainer. But once again, it survived.

"Gordon will never be forgotten," I say. I pick up Ella's sketch of the imaginary Gordon. Making *this* a reality is going to be very cool. I look at Shahid. "What do you think we should use to attach the sunglasses? Duct tape or elastic?"

Shahid's eyes gleam, and he pulls something out of his backpack. "Neither." With a flourish worthy of Gaga Girl, he brandishes a package. "I think we should advance to Velcro."

Acknowledgments

Thank you to authors Diane Tullson and Shelley Hrdlitschka for continuing to share all the imaginations we make real on the page. To Galen and Bela Tweedale, for reading and commenting on an early draft, many thanks, guys. The notion expressed in the story by Ella, that "Life imitates art," must be attributed to Oscar Wilde. Finally, my gratitude to Melanie Jeffs, Orca editor, and all the team at Orca Book Publishers for their excellent work in bringing stories to readers.

Kim Denman is the author of numerous books for youth, including *Rebel's Tag*, *Mirror Image*, *The Shade* and *Perfect Revenge* in the Orca Currents series, and the Governor General's Literary Award nominee, *Me, Myself and Ike*.